Book One

A DOZEN A DAY

FOR GUITAR

Technical Exercises for the Guitar to Be Done Each Day Before Practicing

By Dale Turner

Based on the Best-Selling Piano Series by Edna Mae Burnam

T0082075

PLAYBACK+
Speed • Pitch • Balance • Loop

To access audio, visit:
www.halleonard.com/mylibrary

Enter Code
4914-6725-3354-9745

ISBN 978-1-4234-5126-6

WILLIS MUSIC

EXCLUSIVELY DISTRIBUTED BY

HAL•LEONARD®

Visit Hal Leonard Online at
www.halleonard.com

World headquarters, contact:
Hal Leonard
7777 West Bluemound Road
Milwaukee, WI 53213
Email: info@halleonard.com

In Europe, contact:
Hal Leonard Europe Limited
1 Red Place
London, W1K 6PL
Email: info@halleonardeurope.com

In Australia, contact:
Hal Leonard Australia Pty. Ltd.
4 Lentara Court
Cheltenham, Victoria, 3192 Australia
Email: info@halleonard.com.au

A DOZEN A DAY

A DOZEN A DAY

Many people do exercises each morning before they start school, go to work, or head out for a day at the beach or park. Likewise, guitarists should give their fingers exercises every day BEFORE they begin practicing. That's where this book, *A Dozen a Day*—a book designed for use with any beginning method (or series "book one") for either class or private instruction—comes into play.

As fledgling guitarists begin learning notes on their instruments, they should put these "new" notes to use right away with *fun* technical exercises. This not only helps maintain interest while refining the left/right hand mechanics involved in guitar playing, but it leads to increased playing comfort, improved tone production, and makes it easier to absorb new musical subjects quickly. Though this book was designed to help early-level guitar students develop strong hands and flexible fingers, when used in conjunction with a private teacher, it will also deepen the young guitarist's understanding of chords and their construction (via the "Building Blocks" examples, among others), and help demystify the guitar's complicated fretboard/note layout. At the very least, by book's end, the student will be better equipped to locate the guitar's equivalent of the piano's "white keys" (via the "Alphabet Game" examples, among others).

If this book is being used along with a beginning method (in private lessons or group instruction), realize that most exercises are built from notes the young guitarist is learning to read; the student should be able to locate these notes on his/her fretboards as they enjoy their *A Dozen A Day* exercises. However, several exercises are *purely physical* in nature and will not be "readable" by beginning level guitarists. For this reason, and to speed up the "playing" process in general, a tablature staff accompanies every notated musical example. In most cases, picking instructions and fret-hand fingerings are also included.

NOTE: Students should not try to learn the entire first dozen exercises the first week they study this book! Rather, they should learn two or three exercises and do them each day *before* practicing. When these are mastered, they'll be ready to add another, then another, and keep adding until all twelve can be played perfectly. When the first dozen—or *Group I*—has been mastered and perfected, *Group II* may be introduced in the same manner, and so on for the other groups. Many of these exercises may be transposed to different keys, or shifted up and down the frets to focus on technique within narrowing/widening spans of frets. Enjoy!

— *Dale Turner*

GROUP I

1. Up and Down Track 1

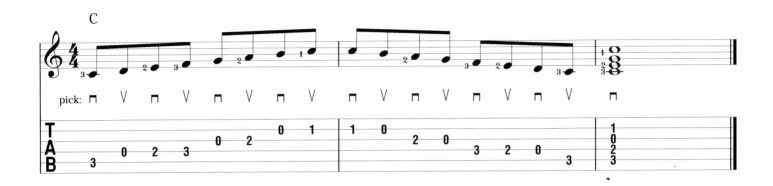

2. Under and Over Track 2

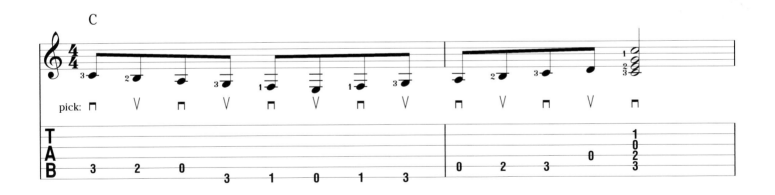

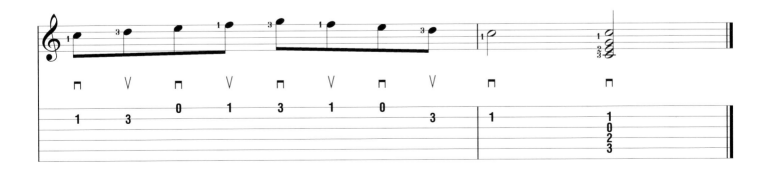

3. Building Blocks

Track 3

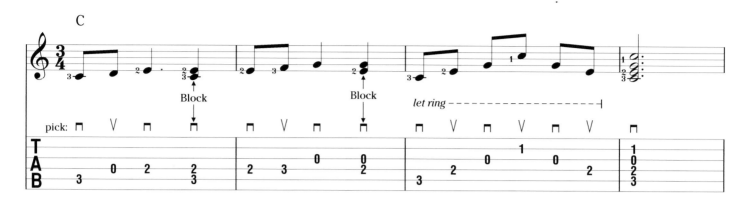

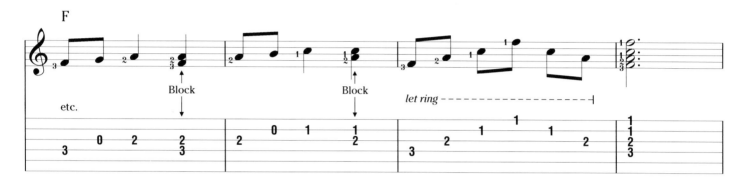

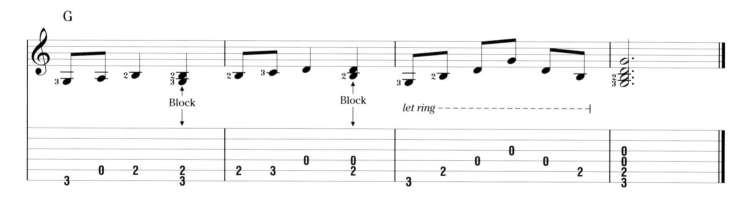

4. Pinky Power

Track 4

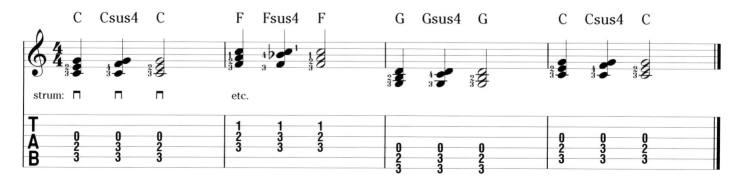

5. Royal Trumpets

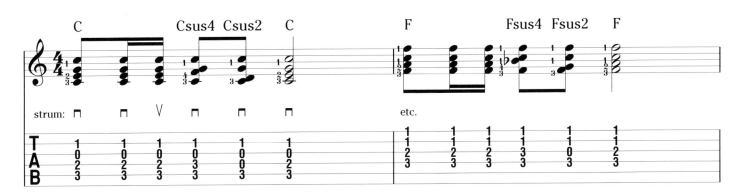

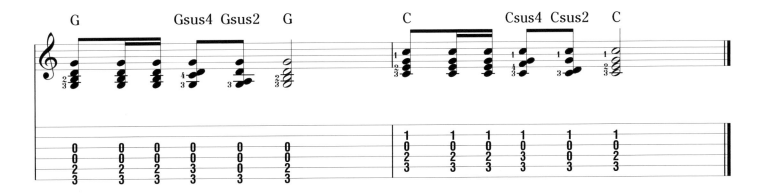

6. Pick 'Em Up and Move 'Em Over

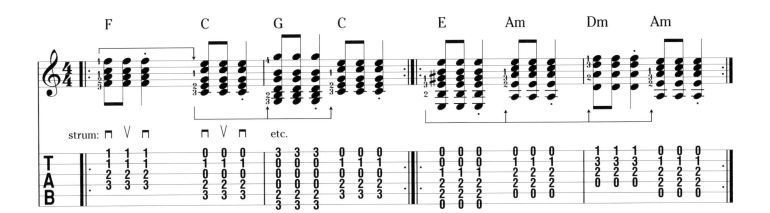

7. Spanish Dance

Track 7

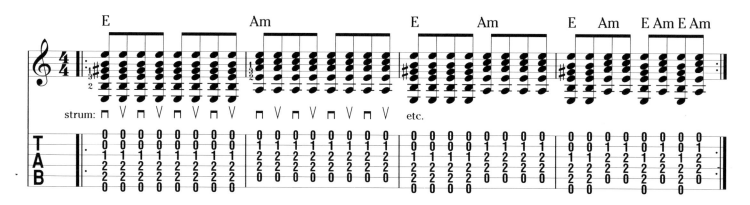

8. Common Ground

Track 8

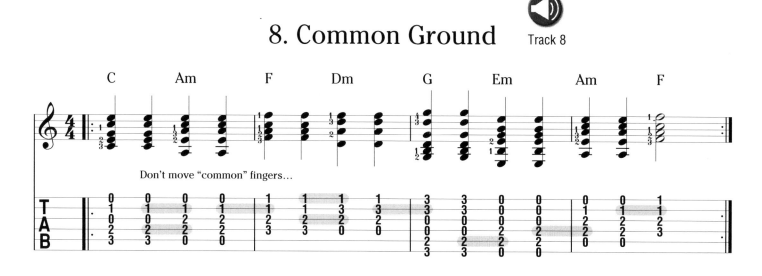

Don't move "common" fingers...

9. Echo

Track 9

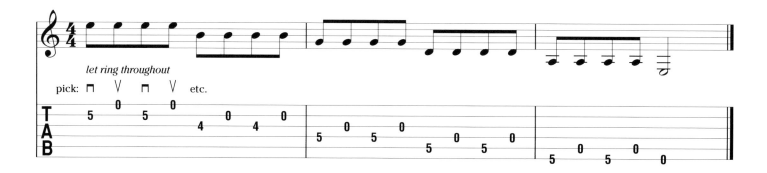

let ring throughout

10. Alphabet Game

Track 10

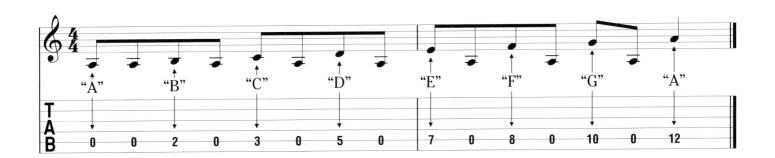

11. Baby Steps

Track 11

12. One-Pick Pony

Track 12

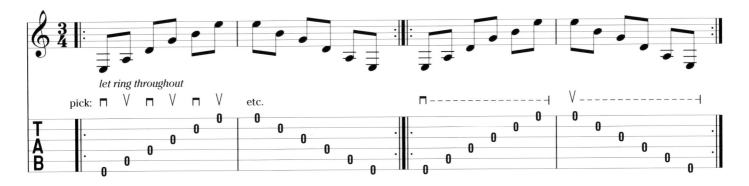

GROUP II

1. Jumping Higher and Higher/Hanging Upside-Down Track 13

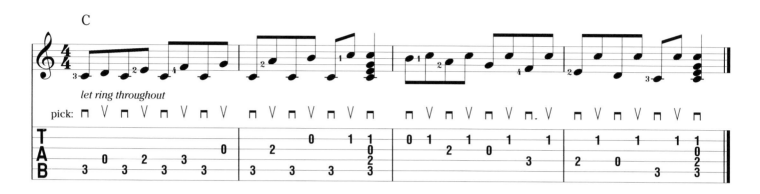

2. Moving Up in the World  Track 14

3. Building Blocks Track 15

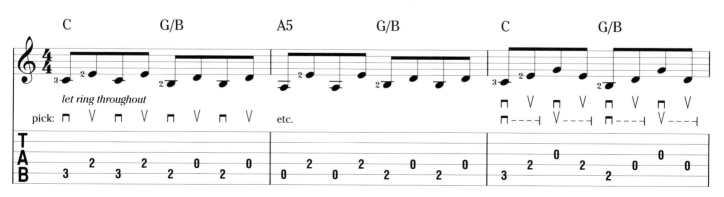

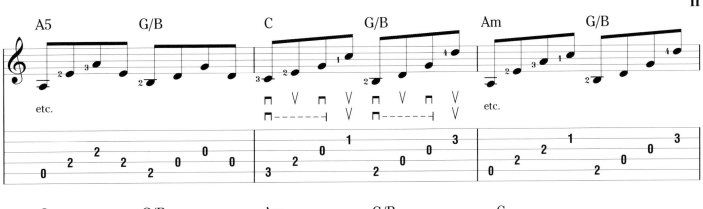

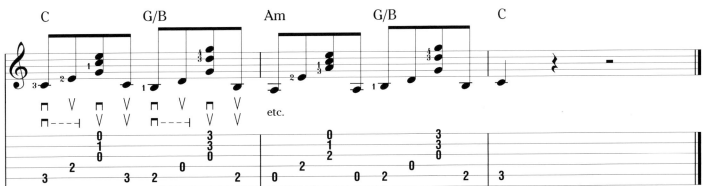

4. Cathedral Bells

Track 16

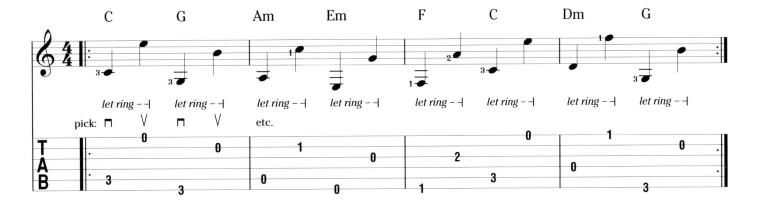

5. Kings and Queens

Track 17

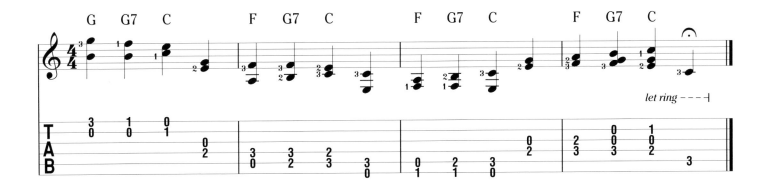

6. Sailing the Seven (Other) Cs

Track 18

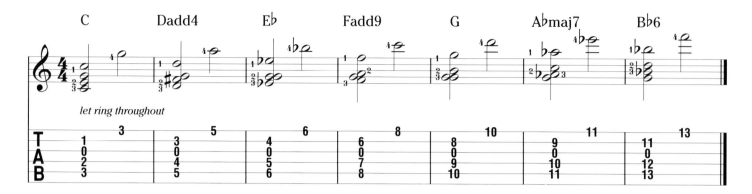

7. Keep 'Em Ringin'

Track 19

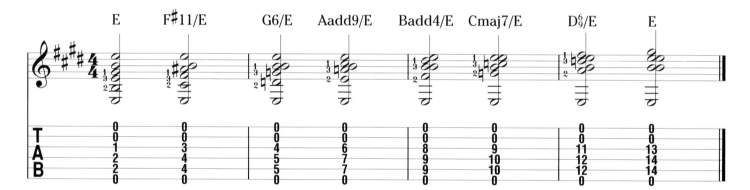

8. Trading Places/Moving Up

Track 20

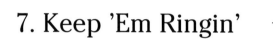
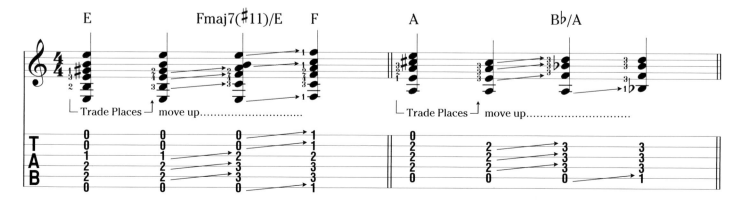

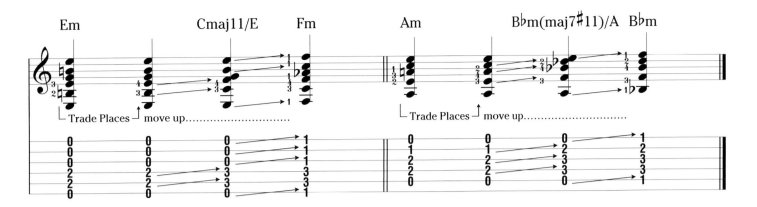

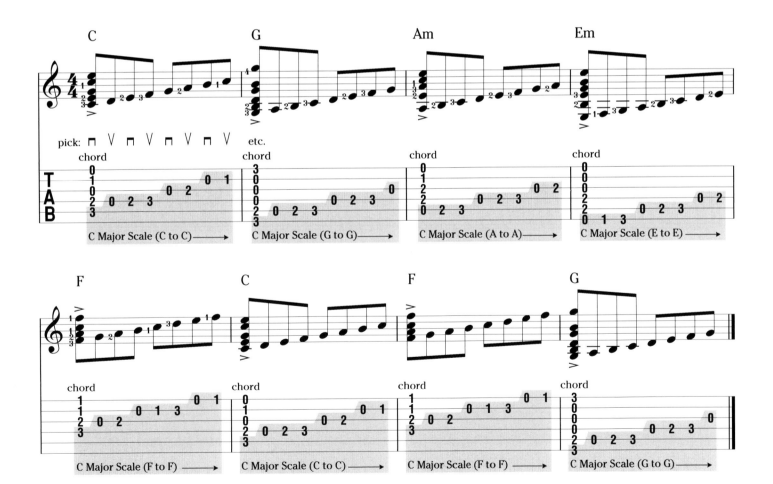

9. Chord/Scale Connection   Track 21

10. Alphabet Game

Track 22

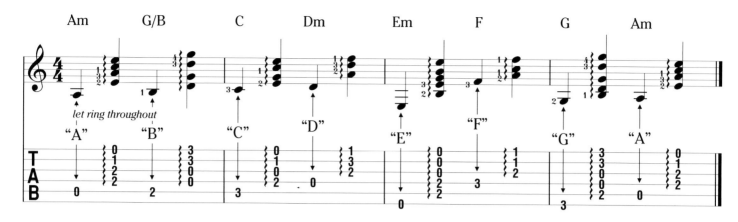

11. Pinched Pair/Spaced Pair

Track 23

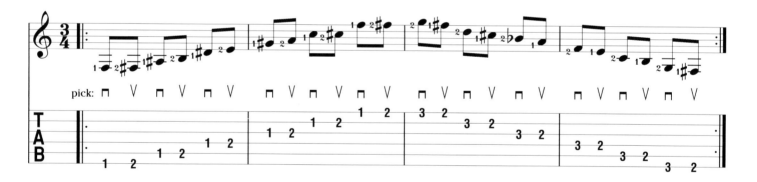

12. Stutter Steps

 Track 24

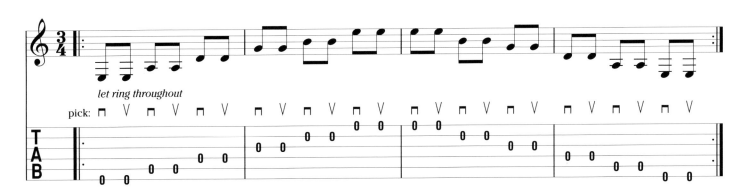

let ring throughout

GROUP III

1. Surrounding the Center

 Track 25

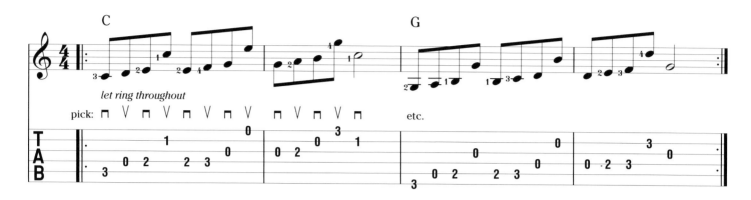

2. Questions and Answers

 Track 26

3. Top Note Lullaby

Track 27

4. Making Popcorn

Track 28

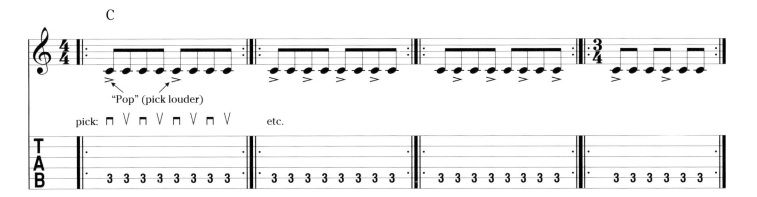

5. Alphabet Game

Track 29

6. Tighten That Grip!

 Track 30

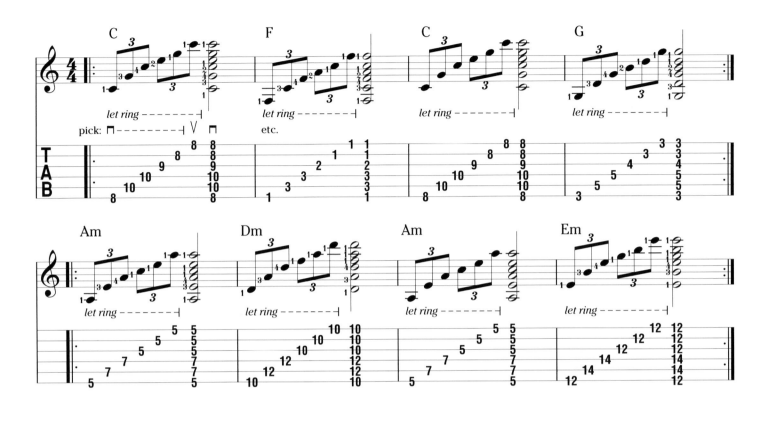

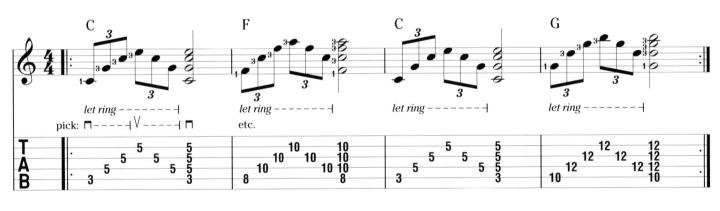

7. Squeeze Play

 Track 31

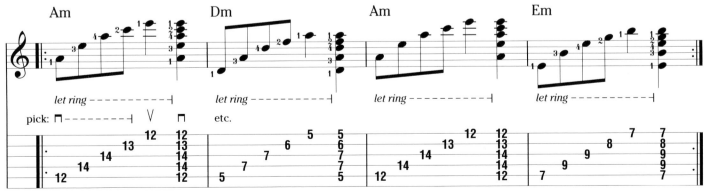

8. Going Deeper

Track 32

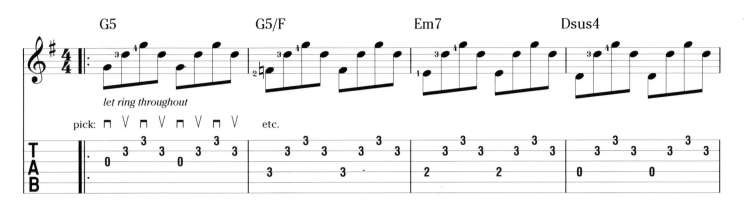

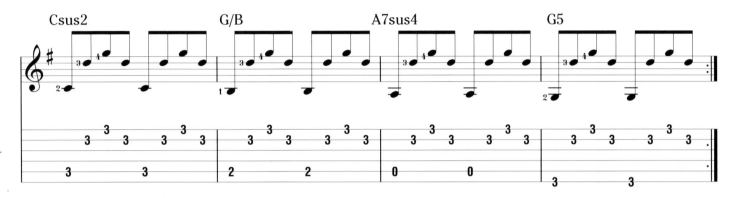

9. Galloping

Track 33

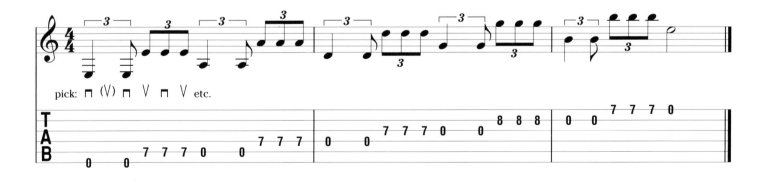

10. Wind Chimes

Track 34

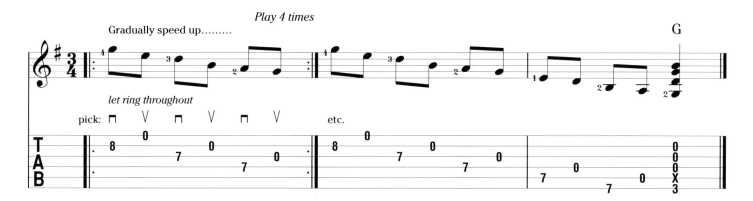

11. Three's a Crowd

Track 35

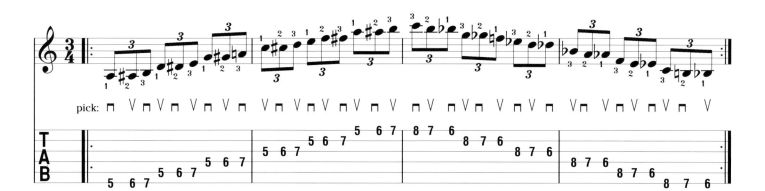

12. Triple Pickle

Track 36

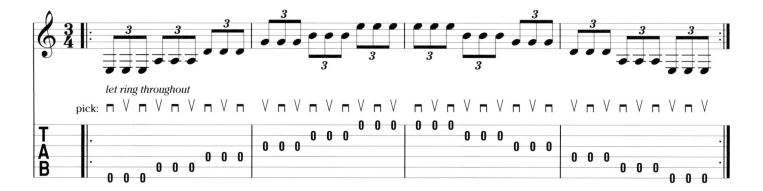

GROUP IV

1. Skipping Track 37

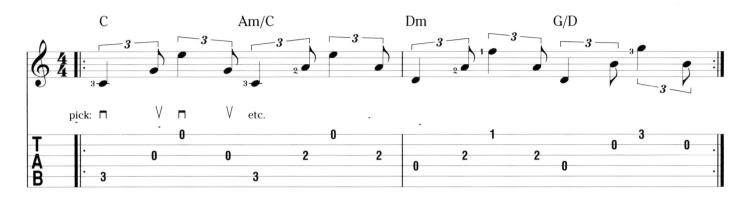

2. Jumping Rope Track 38

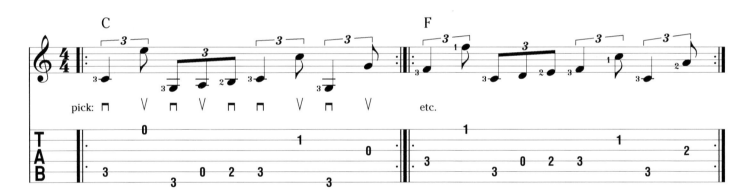

3. Building Blocks Track 39

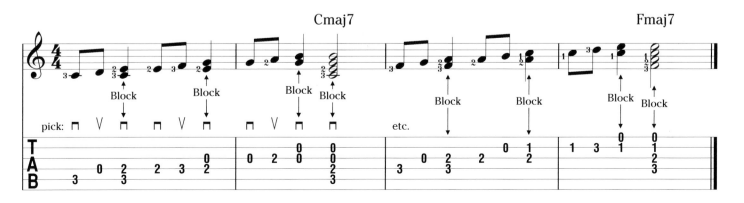

4. Coloring Inside the Lines

Track 40

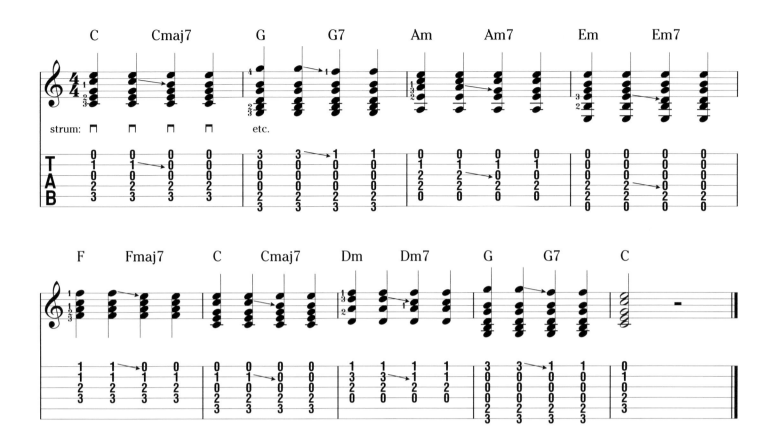

5. Moving on Both Sides

Track 41

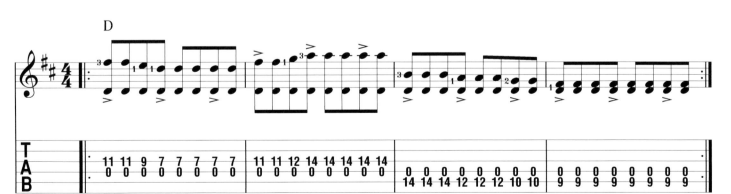

6. Connect the Dots

Track 42

7. Alphabet Game

Track 43

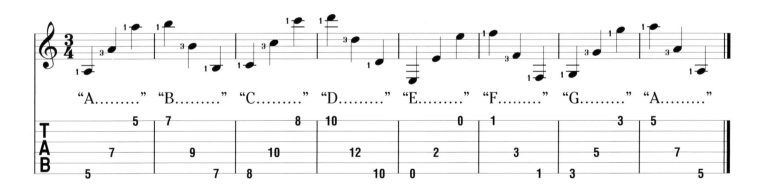

8. Running in Place

 Track 44

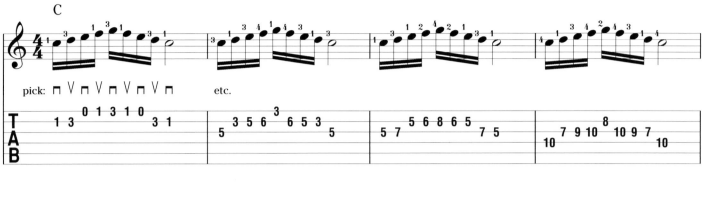

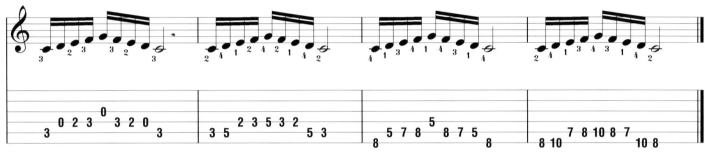

9. Power of Five

 Track 45

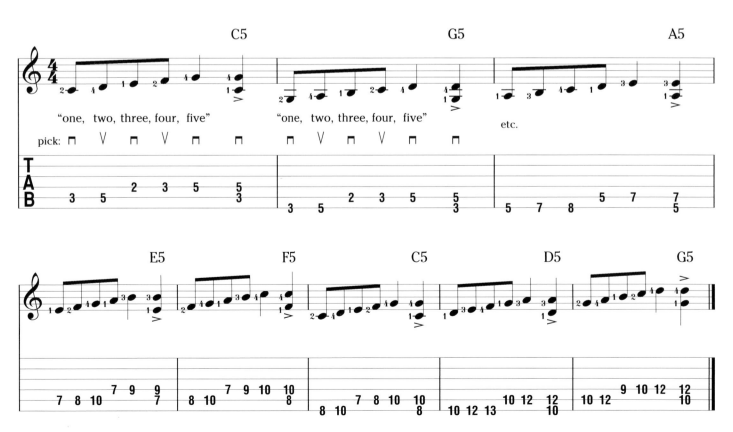

10. Stretch Low, Reach High Track 46

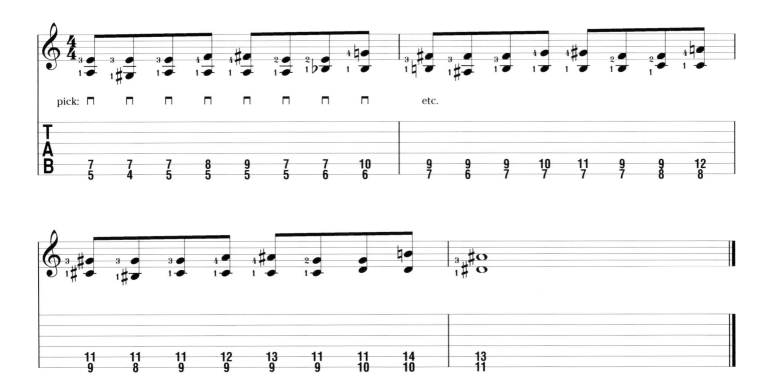

11. Four Fingers Moving Forward (and Backward) Track 47

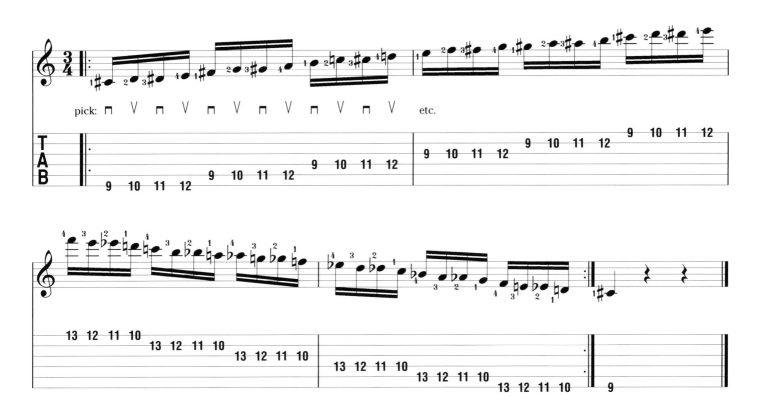

12. Fun with Fours

Track 48

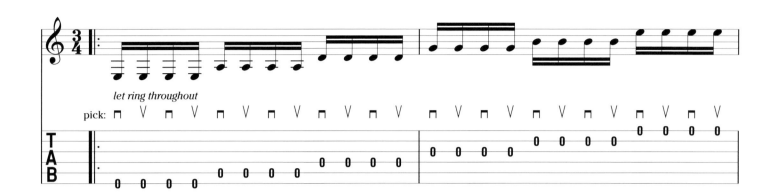

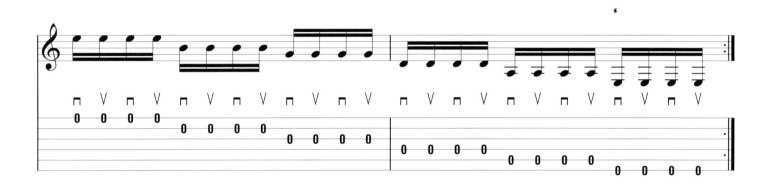

GROUP V

1. Mountain Climbing

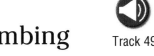
Track 49

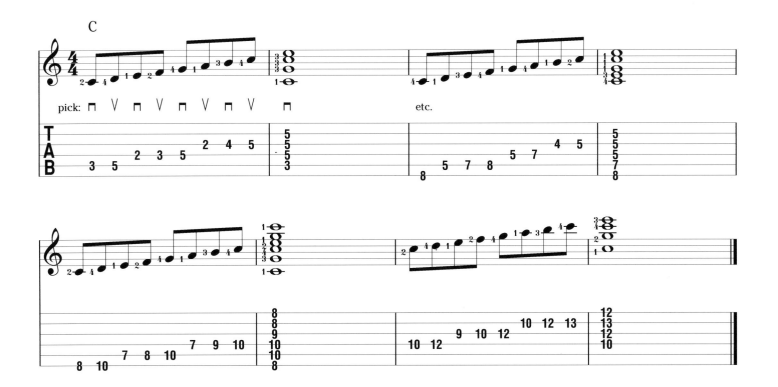

2. Sneaking Around

Track 50

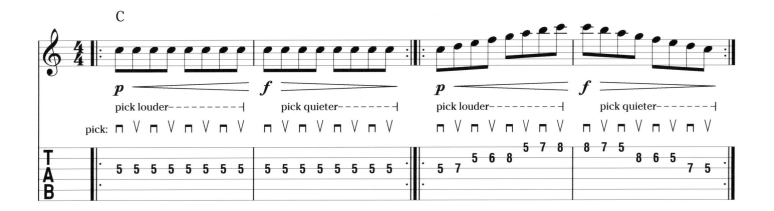

3. Power Picking

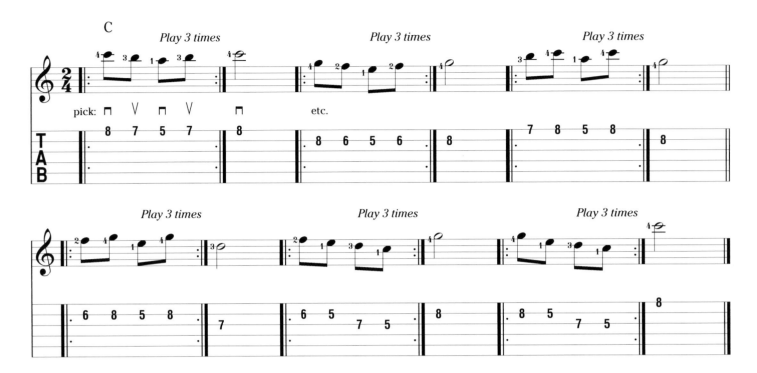

4. Call and Response

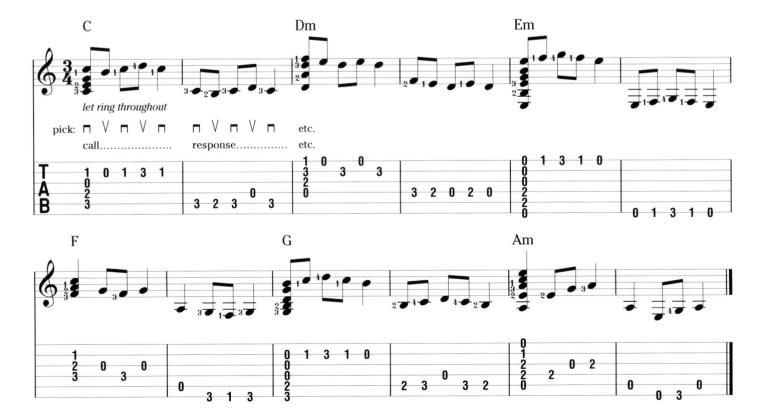

5. Common Ground

Track 53

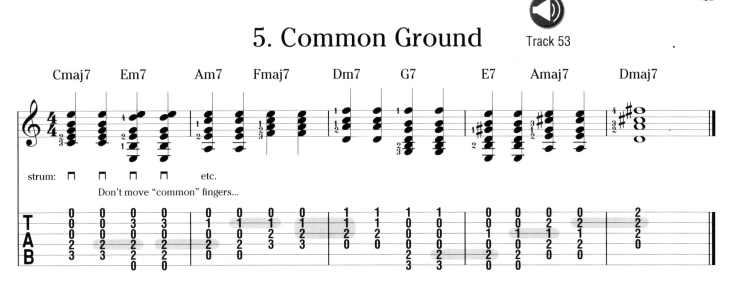

6. Going Home

Track 54

7. 4-2-1 Stretch

Track 55

8. Surf Pickin'

Track 56

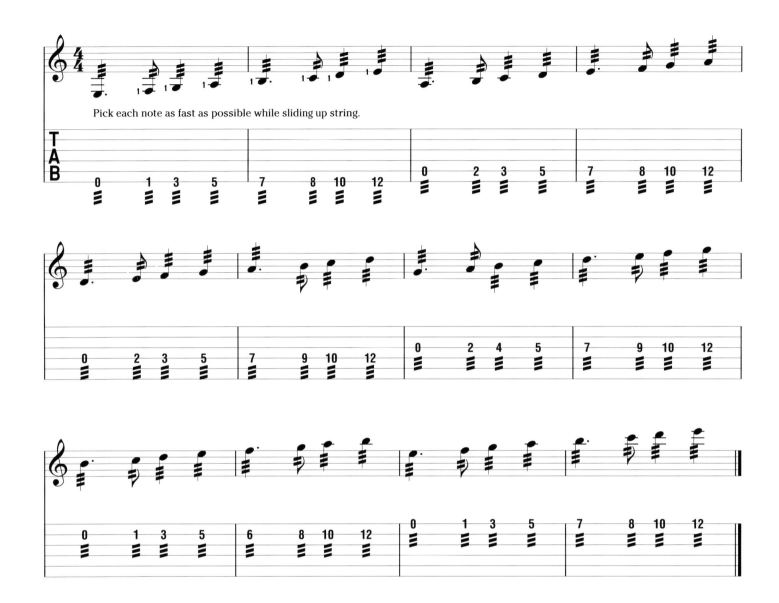

9. Alphabet Game

Track 57

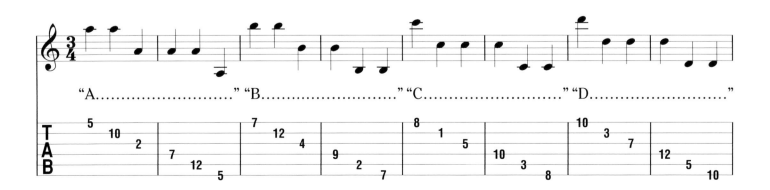

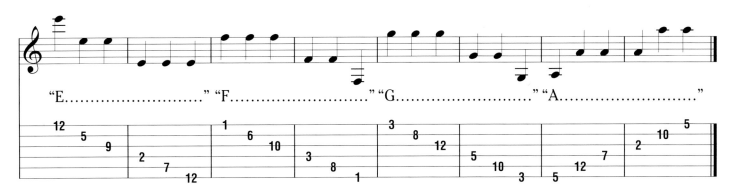

10. Rollercoaster Ride   Track 58

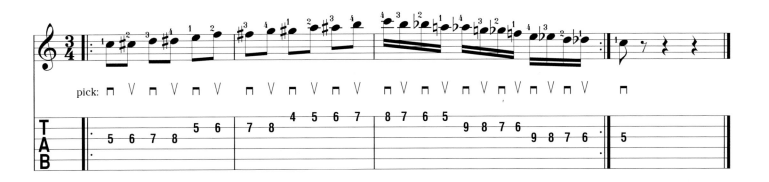

11. Spider   Track 59

12. Open-String Etude

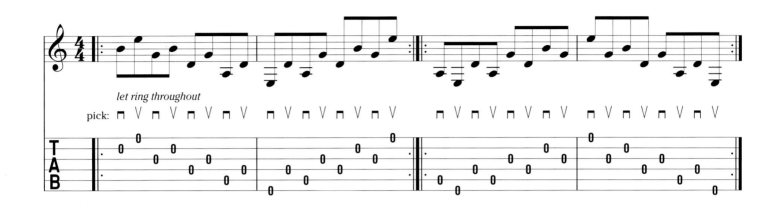

let ring throughout

pick:

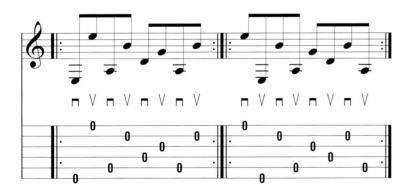